161
WATERFOWLING

SECRETS

TIME-HONORED, FIELD-TESTED
WATERFOWLING TIPS AND ADVICE
FROM DUCKS UNLIMITED MEMBERS

edited by
Matt Young

illustrated by
Lee D. Salber
and Michael DiFrisco

published by
Ducks Unlimited, Inc.
Memphis, Tennessee

161 Waterfowling Tips
©Copyright 1994, Ducks Unlimited, Inc.

ISBN 0-9617279-2-6

The mission of Ducks Unlimited is to fulfill the annual life cycle needs of North American waterfowl by protecting, enhancing, restoring, and managing important wetlands and associated uplands. Since its founding in 1937, DU has raised over $819 million, which has contributed to the conservation of over seven million acres of prime wildlife habitat in all 50 states, each of the Canadian provinces, and key areas of Mexico. In the United States alone, DU has helped to conserve over 700,000 acres of waterfowl habitat. Some 600 species of wildlife live and flourish on DU projects, including many threatened or endangered species.

For membership information, call 1-800-45-DUCKS.

Ducks Unlimited, Inc.
One Waterfowl Way, Memphis, TN 38120

TABLE OF CONTENTS

F O R E W O R D

Being A Better Waterfowler
Improving your hunting skills is an important part of
being a conservationist. Properly identifying ducks,
estimating shooting range, and using a retriever are
integral to conserving our precious waterfowl
resources. Those wondrous birds are what have
drawn so many hunters to Ducks Unlimited, because
there isn't a waterfowler alive who hasn't marveled at
the sights and sounds of a sunrise framed by
silhouetted wildfowl. Through Ducks Unlimited,
waterfowlers have long shown their commitment to
maintaining and restoring the vital habitats that
sustain North America's ducks and geese.

The sporting public can help ensure the continued
success of our wildfowl by passing on the grand
tradition of waterfowling. As a hunter comes to
spend time in a marsh, surrounded by the life that
teems in these environs, he develops both an
understanding and an appreciation for preserving
such important ecosystems. It is out of this close
relationship with the land and its wildlife that life-
long conservationists are born, people who can be
counted on to work diligently to preserve both wild
places and the sporting heritage that goes with them.

Matthew B. Connolly, Jr.
Executive Vice President, Ducks Unlimited, Inc.

INTRODUCTION

When we first placed an advertisement in the January/
February 1994 issue of *Ducks Unlimited* magazine
soliciting waterfowling tips from members to be
compiled in a book, we were astounded by the response.
Within three months after the ad appeared in the
magazine, we received more than 200 submissions from
members throughout the United States and Canada. We
also selected tips from the more than 250 submissions
we had received during the previous year for the "Mixed
Bag" column in the magazine. In the end, we compiled
the 161 best waterfowling tips from almost 1,000
submitted by more than 450 contributors.

The tips cover a wide range of waterfowling topics,
presented in the following chapters: Blinds and
Concealment, Boats, Calls and Calling, Decoys,
Retrievers, Guns and Loads, Safety, Tactics, Waders, and
Miscellaneous Tips. Many were submitted with hand
drawings that served as the basis for the illustrations
appearing in this book. Ducks Unlimited's *161
Waterfowling Secrets* is a testament to the hunting skill
and ingenuity of the Ducks Unlimited membership,
because without their knowledge and expertise, this
book wouldn't have been possible.

Good hunting!
DU Magazine Staff

Blinds & Concealment

From simple goose pits to Barnegat Bay sneak boxes, waterfowlers have devised many ingenious ways to hide themselves from the sharp eyes of wildfowl. Some waterfowlers hunt from blinds with all the comforts of home while others prefer simpler, more utilitarian hides. Regardless of their design and construction, the best blinds are almost invisible against surrounding vegetation and terrain. As hunting pressure has increased in many parts of the country, waterfowl have become increasingly wary of blinds, making thorough concealment essential for success.

1. LIVING BLIND

Many hunters spend a weekend or two each fall cutting willow and oak branches to brush their blind. One weekend last spring, I dug up the rhizomes (roots) of cattails and young willow saplings and planted them in the mud around my blind. They grew well over the summer and made my blind much less conspicuous this season. In the future, a little pruning will be all that is needed to prepare my blind for the hunting season.

Mark Ernst
Bedford, Texas

2. SHALLOW GRAVE

When hunting Canada geese, it's best to place your decoy spread in the center of the field where geese are feeding, rather than beside fence rows. To conceal myself in the middle of a field without building a conspicuous blind, I dig a long shallow pit 20 inches deep, 24 inches wide, and 30 inches long. I spread cornstalks over any loose dirt and place goose decoys on either side of the pit. When geese approach, I simply crouch down in the pit, safely hidden from the gaze of wary honkers.

Glen Gdanski
Woodstock, Ontario

3. MOBILE BLIND

A convenient portable blind for hunting flats or open marsh can be made by nailing camouflage netting to four 5-foot wooden stakes. Nail and tape the camo netting to the stakes making four corners. This light-weight blind can be easily rolled up and carried on foot or in a small skiff.

Joe Bosco
Moss Point, Mississippi

4. BOAT BLIND

Late in the season, puddle ducks often forsake sloughs and potholes for the security of open water. By using a portable boat blind, one has the mobility to find and hunt ducks on big water.

Joe Bosco
Moss Point, Mississippi

5. DETAILS, DETAILS

On mild, sunny days, pay special attention to

concealment. Wear camouflage clothing that blends into the surrounding cover and a turkey hunter's face net. Also, cover your shotgun with camo tape or mesh to reduce glare. By paying attention to these little details, you will have better success when birds do approach your spread on bright, bluebird days.

Doug Odell
Mt. Airy, North Carolina

6. BURLAP SACKS

Many duck hunters don't have a camouflaged duck boat. An easy, inexpensive solution is to use old burlap for concealment. Cut open old burlap bags and camouflage them with black or green spray paint. Drape them over the engine, consoles, gunwales, etc. Canvas or other material can be used, but burlap is much lighter and easier to carry.

George O'Kelley, Jr.
Beaufort, South Carolina

7. SWAMP SEAT

My hunting partner Ron Forster and I developed the "swamp seat" to provide comfortable and stable seating in the marsh. Using the swamp seat one can sit in stability and comfort in up to 16 inches of water. In addition, the swamp seat swivels, allowing a hunter to swing on passing birds without standing up.

It consists of four parts. The rounded plywood seat sits upon a pipe flange with a short nipple which fits inside the aluminum pipe support post. To prevent the sitter from sinking into the mud, a 10-inch, donut-shaped plywood disc fits around the base of the pipe and is secured by metal pins (above and below) that fit through a series of holes drilled through the pipe.

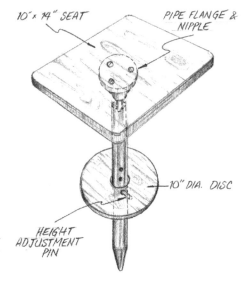

Thomas Fulk
Anacortes, Washington

8. SHIRT COVER

During the past few years, I have used worn-out T-shirts for an outboard motor cover. Simply sew the neck of a T-shirt together. This is a great way to cover an outboard without having to spend money on a custom motor cover.

Kevin Stallard
Highland, Illinois

9. FIRST FROST

If you use willow branches to camouflage your blind, cut them before the first frost. They will retain their leaves much longer.

Terry Lindsay
Athens, Illinois

10. BEAVER PROOF

While hunting Lake Gaston on the North Carolina-Virginia border, we have found it is well worthwhile to cover the posts of our blinds with PVC pipe. This prevents beavers from gnawing on them. This simple step can save a great deal of inconvenience after the blind is completed.

R.L. and Chad Coley
Palmer Springs, Virginia

11. FEED TROUGH

In our neck of the woods, it's not unusual to see Canada geese feeding with livestock. Since the geese are accustomed to seeing feed troughs in fields, my husband and his friends use them as blinds while goose hunting. The geese can't see hunters lying in the troughs, and the guys don't have to lie on the cold, wet ground.

Renee Coon
Red Hook, New York

12. MOCK BLIND

I have discovered a trick for hunting out of blinds brushed with materials not indigenous to your immediate area. I build a few mock blinds 100 yards on either side of my blind. This will make it seem like a natural part of the landscape.

Luke Butler
Lafayette, Louisiana

13. SHOOT SITTING

If you hunt out of a "sit down" blind, take your first shot sitting. Since ducks flare when hunters stand up, this will ensure at least one good shot at decoying ducks.

Luke Butler
Lafayette, Louisiana

14. FLOATING BLIND

If you hunt in an area where water levels fluctuate dramatically, build your blind on a floating platform. Fix two posts through holes cut in the back corners of the platform. This way, the blind can ride up and down as the water level fluctuates, while remaining almost as stable as a fixed blind.

Joseph Wargo
Streator, Illinois

15. CHRISTMAS CAMO

A realistic-looking, durable camouflage material for your blind is artificial Christmas trees. If the limbs are too green in color to match surrounding cover, spray paint them olive drab. I use the limbs to cover the sides and the roof. I also nail them to stakes and place them in the surrounding shallow water to further break the outline of the blind. Used Christmas trees can be bought cheaply after the holidays. Check newspaper classified sections, department store clearance sales, and garage sales.

J.C. Ingram
Sycamore, Illinois

16. CONTACT PAPER

When using metal conduit for blind frames, I cover it with brown or green contact paper rather than paint. It is much more durable. When using gray or black PVC pipe, I simply sandblast it to reduce its shine rather than painting it.

Greg Goda
Butler, Pennsylvania

17. BAMBOO CURTAINS

Split bamboo patio curtains popular in the 1950s make very good camouflage for a blind surrounded by cattails or tall grass. They can usually be found for sale at low cost at flea markets or garage sales.

Greg Goda
Butler, Pennsylvania

18. CAMO UMBRELLA

Your hunting buddies will be laughing the first time you show up at the marsh with a large camouflage umbrella, but once it starts raining, you'll find you have company underneath it. The umbrella can also serve as a sunshade on those bright, early October days. As long as you don't move it, ducks will decoy to your spread.

Don Davidson
Klamath Falls, Oregon

19. GRASS BLIND

A light, inconspicuous portable blind can be made from plastic fencing material used for commercial fish farms. Staple the fencing to four or five light, wooden rods, then tightly weave native grass or cattails through the openings in the fencing. While hunting, place the blind amidst matching cover. The blind can be firmly anchored by driving the rods into the mud. At the end of the hunt, carefully roll up the blind and stow it in your boat.

Duncan Campbell
Fredericton, New Brunswick

20. TREE PRUNERS

All a mobile hunter needs to quickly create an effective blind is a pair of hand tree pruners. Find a dense clump of bushes at the water's edge and prune an opening in the middle for you and your dog. Remove branches that may block your swing while shooting and prune holes in the front to look out.

Eldon Belyea
Fredericton, New Brunswick

21. REFLECTOR TACK

To help you find your well-hidden blind on dark or foggy mornings, place a small reflector tack on the front of the blind. With a powerful spotlight, you will be able to locate your blind from afar even in dismal weather.

Brad Hedtke
Waupaca, Wisconsin

22. CLOTHES PINS

I always include a half-dozen spring-loaded clothes pins in the gear bucket that I carry to the blind. These inexpensive pins can be used to hold camouflage netting, branches, and cattails on the sides of my blind.

Harold Podolske
Alexandria, Minnesota

Boats

Waterfowlers have pursued their sport aboard a wide array of crafts—each specially designed to weather any kind of water inhabited by wildfowl. Customizing these crafts has become something of a time-honored tradition among waterfowlers, people who take pride in what has become an art form of sorts. Here, then, are ideas that will help you turn your boat into a comfortable and safe home on the water.

23. PIPE DREAM

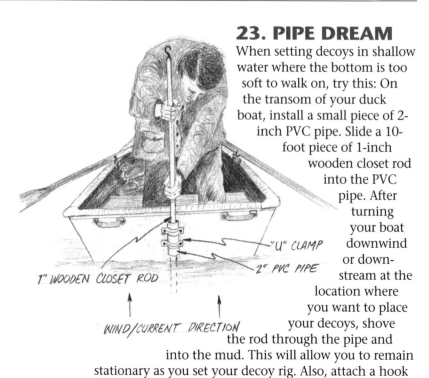

"U" CLAMP

2" PVC PIPE

1" WOODEN CLOSET ROD

WIND/CURRENT DIRECTION

When setting decoys in shallow water where the bottom is too soft to walk on, try this: On the transom of your duck boat, install a small piece of 2-inch PVC pipe. Slide a 10-foot piece of 1-inch wooden closet rod into the PVC pipe. After turning your boat downwind or down-stream at the location where you want to place your decoys, shove the rod through the pipe and into the mud. This will allow you to remain stationary as you set your decoy rig. Also, attach a hook on one end of the 10-foot pole, so you can use it to retrieve decoys.

Tom Leef
Marion Station, Maryland

24. GUNWALE COVERS

Covering the gunwales of your boat can serve many purposes: it makes your boat quieter, helps protect your gun barrels, and breaks up the outline of the boat. Check with your local fire department to see if they might have a piece of unusable fire hose. If they do, they will be happy to get rid of it. Remove the fittings if they haven't already done so and return them. With a sharp knife, split the entire hose lengthwise. Place the split hose over the gunwales of the boat and secure to seat braces with plastic ties.

Bernie Elhard
Northome, Minnesota

25. ICEBREAKERS

If you find yourself breaking ice with your boat paddles during the late season, here's a way to keep your paddles from splitting during tough duty. Coat the blades of your paddles with fiberglass that is available at most hardware stores. This will strengthen them and add life to their use.

Michael Richart
Galion, Ohio

26. TIPPY CANOE

Tippy boat problems can be eliminated by using this simple method. Place four 2x4s into the lake or marsh bottom at each corner of your boat or skiff. Then attach a 1/2-inch eye screw on the inside of each of the 2x4s, level with the top edge of the boat. A rope or light chain can then be fastened between the eyes across both the front and back of the boat. When tied tightly, your boat won't rock or tip when you stand to shoot. To keep the boat from squeaking against the 2x4s, tack a 4x12-inch piece of indoor-outdoor carpet on the inside of the 2x4s. Use a 12-inch-long piece of carpet in case of water level fluctuations.

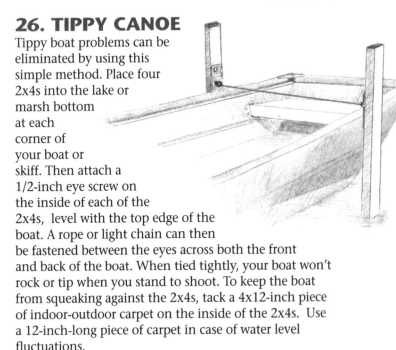

Bill Lange
Iron Ridge, Wisconsin

27. TIED UP

When hunting from a boat, do not lift anchor when retrieving ducks. Instead, untie the rope from the boat and attach it to a float—such as an extra decoy or large plastic jug. When you return, you will be able to set up in the same position. This will enable you to resume hunting faster, especially in rough water.

Hal Hutchinson
Evart, Michigan

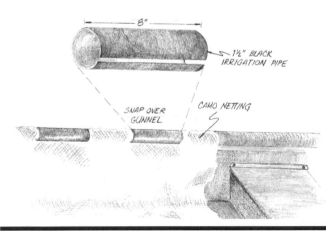

28. SECURING PADDLES

When float hunting from a canoe or small boat, tie the paddles to the side of the boat on a 2- or 3-yard piece of cord. Then, when you spot ducks, just drop the paddle into the water and ready your gun. This saves time and eliminates the noise of hurrying to place the paddles inside the boat.

James L. Nelson
Newark, Ohio

29. TABLE THE ISSUE

To create a handy table in your motorized duck boat and camouflage your orange or red gas tank at the same time, build a plywood box with a hinged lid that is just large enough for a 6-gallon outboard gas tank. Drill or router holes in each end for carrying and for running the gas line through. Screw or nail 1x1-inch pieces of wood around the top edge of the lid so that your thermos, coffee cup, shotgun shells, and the like won't slide off onto the wet floor of the boat. Paint the box your favorite camouflage pattern.

Steve Swentkofske
Cohasset, Minnesota

30. BLIND ATTACHMENT

Attaching blind material to a boat can often be a hassle. Here's a painless and inexpensive way, however, to do just that. Buy 8 feet of 1 1/2-inch black irrigation pipe from your local hardware store. Cut the pipe into 8-inch sections and then cut the sections lengthwise. These sections will snap over almost any boat gunwale, holding camouflage netting and other material snugly in place.

David Desrochers
Pontiac, Michigan

31. NO LOST OARS

To prevent your oars from slipping out of the oarlocks while hunting or during transport, attach a heavy-gauge piece of wire to a heavy cord and tie them through the hole in the bottom of the oarlock.

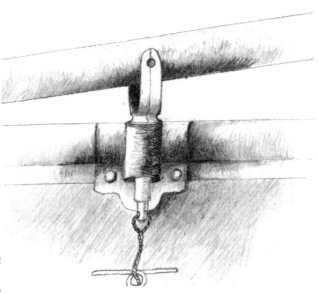

Jerry Thompson
New Ulm,
Minnesota

32. HOOK UPS

If you're tired of tying and untying a cold, stiff rope when securing your boat to a blind or tree, try using a snap hook on the end of the ropes that are attached to your hunting boat. Also, by installing eye hooks on the blind, you can easily hook and unhook the boat when you need to quickly retrieve cripples or when you want to leave for the day.

Eddie Jenkins
Shreveport, Louisiana

33. ARTISTIC CAMO

A great way to put a realistic camo paint job on your duck boat or other equipment is to use pieces of tree branches with leaves as stencils for spray paint. Hold the natural stencil material near the boat and make a pass with the spray can, creating a faint, shadowy outline. Try to make shadowy images rather than hard, crisp impressions. Move around the boat, making spray patterns at different angles and with different colors. The end result will be a highly realistic camouflage that is much more aesthetic than most of the paint jobs you see at the local boat landing.

Larry Robinson
Lupton, Michigan

34. EXTRA FLOTATION

When you have finished using your decoys for the day, pack them up in their bags and tie the bags shut. Should your craft capsize, these bags will serve as extra flotation devices.

Joseph Last
Green Bay, Wisconsin

Calls & Calling

For many hunters, calling is the most rewarding part of waterfowling. Few events are as dramatic as hailing a high flock of ducks with a highball and watching them turn and cup their wings in unison as the sound reaches them through the howling wind. Much more than an effective method of bringing waterfowl into range, calling enables hunters to interact directly with the fascinating wild birds that draw them to the marshes each autumn.

35. DENTAL FLOSS

After a season of waterfowling, calls often get dirty and tend to stick. Try flossing the reed with unwaxed dental floss to clean out the dirt and other debris. By not taking the call apart while cleaning it, you won't have to tune it again.

Jeff Lawrence
Oxford, Mississippi

36. BOTTLE CAP

An inexpensive wood duck call can be made from two beer bottle caps. Simply seal the serrated edges of both caps together with hot glue or five-minute epoxy and drill a 1/4-inch hole through the center of both caps.

$1/4''$

To reproduce the whistle of a woody, hold the call against your teeth with your lips and suck in. By varying your air intake, you can vary the tone to closely imitate a woody on the water.

Roger Letendre
Dover, New Hampshire

37. CALL CASE

While goose and duck hunting, one tends to mistreat equipment pretty badly. Consequently, I made a carrying case to protect my favorite duck and goose calls while going to and from the marsh. The case consists of a 1-foot piece of 2-inch PVC pipe, sealed by two removable end caps. This enables me to carry my calls to the blind without worrying about them getting wet, muddy, or crushed. PVC pipe and end caps can be purchased at most hardware stores for less than six dollars.

Nelson, Wilkinson
Rensselaer, New York

38. TWO-IN-ONE

Clamping a mallard call and a pintail whistle together eliminates a lot of fumbling and unnecessary movement in the blind when working ducks. First, line up the top end of each call and wrap the barrels of both calls with friction tape. Then, with a 4-inch hose clamp, join the calls together. If a spacer is needed, place a piece of wine cork to fit between the calls, and tighten the clamp. Then both calls can be controlled at once.

Dave MacGillivray
Concord, California

39. KEEP MUM

Having trouble decoying mallards and other ducks late in the season? Try not calling at all. Often ducks have become so call-shy by the end of the season they will flare at the first quack, even from a real duck. If you must call, try softly blowing a teal or wigeon whistle.

Tommy Talbot
Iowa, Louisiana

40. DRY OUT

Most duck and goose calls have wooden tone channels that trap moisture. As a result, they will often freeze in cold weather. Therefore, the night before you go hunting, take your calls apart and place them by a heating vent in your home or hunting camp. By doing so, you will dry your calls, thus helping to ensure they will function properly when that first big flock of mallards appears at dawn.

Travis Callis
Hecker, Illinois

41. SCARE TACTIC

When circling ducks begin to land out of range, I keep them in the air by blowing a long, loud blast on my call followed by a regular comeback call series (e.g., Quuaacckk!! Quack, Quack, Quack, Quick, Qck). This will often cause the landing ducks to pull up and circle around one more time. I have found this practice is especially valuable when competing with live ducks sitting on the water nearby.

Terry Franklin
Bixby, Oklahoma

42. CALLING TAPE

How does your duck calling sound? If you are a beginning duck hunter or a seasoned veteran, you can improve your calling by listening to yourself. This can be accomplished by recording your calling with a tape recorder. Listen for weaknesses in your repertoire, then practice to improve them.

Matthew Johnson
Lawrence, Kansas

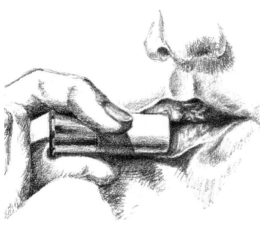

43. SHELL CALL

A very good wood duck call can be made from a spent 20-gauge shotgun shell hull. First, cut off the plastic casing one inch from the brass. Then, place the shell in the corner of your mouth and blow across the open end. This causes the air to circulate within the shell, creating a sound like that of a wood duck. With practice, the tone can be raised and lowered by regulating your breath.

Chuck Howell
Macon, Georgia

44. FOG CALL

When hunting geese in the fog, use your calls intermittently. Call, then listen for a minute or two, then call again. Geese flying in fog are usually very quiet,

listening for calls to guide them through the soupy mist
to a safe resting place.

Kenny Hebert
Lake Charles, Louisiana

45. TAPE IT

To keep your call in one piece and reduce the glare from
plastic or varnished wood, cover it with cloth-backed
camo tape. Be sure the reed assembly is tightly sealed
before taping it.

Mark DesRoches
Kingston, Ontario

46. RUBBER CEMENT

Many times I have been in the field or marsh and lost
the stopper (bottom half) of my call. After having this
happen to an expensive call, I found a way to keep my
new call in one piece. Just put a little rubber cement
around the end of the stopper, just behind the cork. The
call won't come apart accidentally, and you can still take
it apart to adjust the reed.

Jason McCabe
Milwaukie, Oregon

NANCY COX

Decoys

Since Native American hunters
fashioned the first crude replicas of
ducks from woven reeds more than
8,000 years ago, decoys have been an
indispensable waterfowling tool. During
the glory days of American waterfowling, rich decoy-making traditions
evolved in many regions where master
carvers produced cedar and cork blocks
that are now collected as works of art.
Even today, with dozens of durable,
light, and realistic decoys to choose
from, waterfowlers continue to search
for better decoy designs and ways to
deploy them.

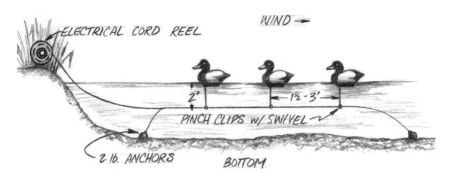

47. DECOY LINE

Like many duck hunters, we use a line system for our decoys. When deployed, our decoy line is anchored at either end by 2-pound weights. We attach our decoys to the metal swivels on the trotline with pinch clips. Each decoy has a 2-foot length of cord that enables the main decoy line to suspend 2 feet under the surface, making it easier for dogs to maneuver around and harder for circling ducks to see. We store our decoy line on a plastic electrical cord reel that can be wound by hand. To pick up our decoys, we simply reel in the main line and detach each decoy as it is brought on shore or into the boat.

Bill McCann
Hamlaile, Minnesota

48. OLD RELIABLE

In today's world of full-bodied and shell goose decoys, the inexpensive, yet effective silhouette decoy has been somewhat forgotten. But these decoys make a very cost effective way to increase your decoy spread. Just set your full-bodied dekes on the periphery of the spread and your silhouettes in the interior.

Another tip when using silhouette goose decoys is to place them facing in various directions. This will create an illusion of movement to geese passing overhead.

Mark DesRoches
Kingston, Ontario

49. CONFIDENCE DEKES

Sometimes confidence decoys can make a difference in your decoy rig, especially in areas that receive a great deal of hunting pressure. We have found that placing a few seagull decoys at the head of our rig can help decoy wary ducks. They are highly visible, and seagulls frequently associate with waterfowl. However, don't place gull dekes downwind of your set because decoying ducks don't like to pass over species other than their own.

Ernest Boynton
Hampden, Maine

50. DECOY REPAIR

I use a piece of black polypropylene rope and a lighter to repair my decoys that have been hit by stray pellets. I simply melt the end of the rope with a lighter and dab the molten plastic in the holes, creating a long-lasting seal.

John Gryn
Bay Shore, New York

51. LANDING DEKES

I made landing goose decoys out of 30- to 50-gallon barrels and feeder goose heads. Cut the body and wings from the side of a plastic barrel. Then, attach the wings and the feeder head to the main body with machine screws.

Jerry Kaufmann
Holy Cross, Iowa

52. SECOND WEIGHT

A decoy cord floating on the surface will attract ducks' attention like a red flag. I've tried to use monofilament line, but I can't even untangle my fishing reel in broad daylight, let alone 15 feet of mono wrapped around a decoy at 5 a.m. To hide my decoy strings from passing ducks, I attach a small weight about a foot down on each decoy cord. This secondary weight holds the line down and out of sight.

Tom Leef
Marion Station, Maryland

53. DRAG RINGS

I have found that the circular drag rings attached to old farm planters and drills make excellent decoy weights. They are made of a rust-proof alloy and conveniently fit over the bill and heads of decoys for tangle-free storage and transport. You can often get them free-for-the-asking from many farmers or buy them cheap from junk dealers who handle farm implements.

Alan Kruse
Middleton, Iowa

54. DECOY GRAPPLE

I have devised a way of retrieving decoys from shore. Insert four or five long screws into a 6-ounce lead sinker at different angles, leaving about 3/4 inch protruding from the weight. Then, tie the weight to 40 feet of line. Store the line rolled up on a stick or kite string reel. Throw the weight beyond each decoy and retrieve the line with your hands, snagging the decoy lines. This enables someone without a boat to deploy a small spread on a pond that is too deep to wade. This is much more feasible than training your Lab to retrieve decoys.

Raymond Tameo
Attleboro, Massachusetts

55. LIQUID STEEL

When some of my decoys inadvertently take a few pellet hits, I repair them with liquid steel, sold in a tube. Simply fill the holes with liquid steel. Then, after it hardens, sand away the excess, and touch it up with paint. Many times, this has saved me the expense of buying new decoys.

Jerry Rohloff
Schofield, Wisconsin

56. BAG 'EM

Given the current price of today's full-bodied goose decoys, every step should be taken to prolong their life. Although I keep my 150 decoys in a custom trailer, they still take a beating while bouncing down farm roads. To protect each decoy from losing paint while rubbing against other decoys, I cover them with 40-gallon lawn bags. While this takes an extra 10 to 15 minutes at the beginning and end of each hunt, it has saved my decoys from much abuse and kept them looking like new.

Matthew Odle
Lehi, Utah

57. GOOSE FLAGS

To add movement to my goose spread, I place several "flags" throughout my spread. These inexpensive decoys can be fashioned by stapling black rags to hand-painted stakes made from wood or plastic. When the wind blows, the rags flutter much like the movement of feeding geese.

Jay Knysch
Forest Park, Illinois

58. MIXED SPREAD

To add diversity to your spread, mix in a dozen or so green-winged teal decoys with your mallards and pintails. I rig three together with a 6-ounce lead weight. I place about 18 in a tight bunch in front of my blind. When ducks are circling my main spread, I peep softly with a teal whistle. I have found that teal and big ducks really respond to this arrangement.

Mark Ernst
Bedford, Texas

59. ANTIFREEZE

For two seasons now, we have improved our early morning success for geese by spraying my field decoys with windshield wiper antifreeze. This removes the frost and dries quickly. We apply the windshield fluid with a 2-gallon bug spray container. This won't harm the decoys, but be sure to restrain over-zealous retrievers that may try to lick recently sprayed decoys.

Allen Draper
Pekin, Illinois

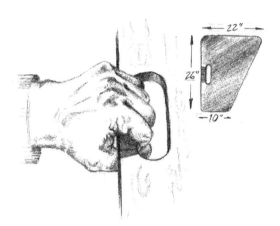

60. WOODEN WING

Waving large black flags will attract the attention of geese that are far away, but will often alarm birds circling the decoys. A more subtle way to add movement to your spread is to use a fiberglass or plywood wing (about 22 x 26 x 10 inches). By raising, wobbling, and then lowering the wing, hunters can attract the attention of circling geese without spooking them.

Marlin Rautzhan
Sinking Spring, Pennsylvania

61. FAMILY GROUPS

When hunting refuge-wise geese, you can improve your success by arranging your decoys into small family groups rather than in one or two large flocks. Scatter these groups across a large area, leaving plenty of room between them. These small clusters of decoys resemble geese resting on a refuge.

Todd Ross
Earlham, Iowa

62. BLACK FELT

To add realism to your Canada goose field decoys, cover their heads and necks with black felt. The felt shines in the sunlight just like the feathers of real geese.

Mark DesRoches
Kingston, Ontario

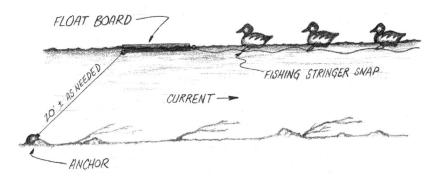

63. FLOAT BOARDS

When we hunt the Susquehanna River in low water conditions, a normal decoy line and anchor will work fine, but when the river rises and current becomes swift, we use a rig called "float boards".

The float board, a 3-foot-long, flat-black piece of plywood, takes the brunt of the current so decoys can float naturally behind it. The board is anchored by a weight attached to a heavy cord. As many as a dozen decoys can be strung out behind the board. Decoys are attached to metal swivels on the decoy line with metal fishing stringer clamps. We place several lines of decoys beside one another, so the final arrangement is quite convincing. It works equally well for geese and divers.

Bill Lawton
Sunbury, Pennsylvania

64. TOUCH UP

Are you interested in making your greenheads stand out? Paint the raised area of the neck and the side of the head with yellowish-green enamel paint. This gives the heads an iridescent appearance, making them far more visible from afar.

Gary Riner
Corryton, Tennessee

65. LIKE NEW

To restore the natural-looking shine on your old
weathered decoys, spray a coat of glossy or satin finish
polyurethane on them after you have washed and dried
them. Polyurethane spray can usually be purchased at
your local hardware or paint store.

Pitt Pittman
Picayune, Mississippi

66. DECOY DIVERSITY

When ducks get wild, try adding a little variety to your
decoys. Mix a few feeders and sleepers with your decoys,
and to really fool that wary old suzy, try a great blue
heron decoy as a sentinel.

Jimmy Jennings
Lepanto, Arkansas

BEFORE

67. LIVING COLOR

For late season hunting for goldeneyes and
old squaws, recycle your old bluebill decoys
by painting them with white latex paint on the
sides and underneath the eyes. This is a cheap and
quick way to make new decoys from the old.

Charles Cooper
Brighton, Ontario

AFTER

68. TEXAS RAGS

Since we live in a motor home, space and
weight are an important consideration as we
follow the waterfowl south in the fall. Therefore, we rely
on Texas rag decoys used with dowel rods. In the field,
each one of us carries 500 decoys secured on a packboard
with bungee straps. We modified our packboards to carry
more gear by extending the vertical uprights 4 feet. The
bungee straps compress the rags into a transportable
bundle. To help us see while walking in the dark, we
wear headlamps.

When we reach the hunting area, we tie a knot in
the corner of each rag to form a head and drape it over
the end of a 16-inch dowel rod driven into the ground.
With every member of the hunting party assisting, a
massive spread of decoys can be deployed in a
surprisingly short period of time. Practice helps, too.

John Kent
Anchorage, Alaska

69. RUBBER BANDS

Stray, rattling decoy weights used to drive me crazy before I figured out a way to secure them during transport. First, go to your tire repair shop and ask for an old tire inner tube. Usually, they are glad to give them away. Next, cut the inner tube into 3/8-inch strips, resembling large rubber bands. Then, tie the rubber bands to your decoy weights. This will enable you to firmly secure weights to your decoys by wrapping the rubber bands around the heads, keels, or tails, thus reducing paint scratching and noise caused by loose weights.

Todd Lawson
Franklin, Tennessee

70. TAKE CARE

In very cold weather, don't haphazardly throw out your decoys. They will get splashed with water that will freeze. When the sun comes out, the ice on the decoys will shine, spooking circling ducks. Therefore, carefully place your decoys on the water when it's bitter cold.

Brad Griffin
DU Greenwing
Athens, Alabama

71. KIDDY SLED

My hunting partner and I purchased two children's sleds for carrying a heavy load of goose decoys through deep snow. We use rubber straps to firmly hold our goose shells and thermoses in place during transport. Paint the sleds camouflage or white. You can also lie down on the sleds in wet snow or use them as headrests.

Greg Rice
Coshocton, Ohio

72. FLUTTERING RAGS

To improve my success while guiding hunters for greater snow geese in Maryland, I developed the ultimate method of adding movement to my decoy spread. I attach 30 white rag decoys to a 150-foot line tied to the top of a 10-foot pole used for a winger decoy in the middle of my decoy spread. When a flock of snows approaches, I pull the line up and down in an undulating manner. The rags on the line will rise and fall just like fluttering geese looking for an opening to land. Keep doing this until the geese are within about 50 yards, then grab your gun. This works equally well on a smaller scale while hunting diving ducks from a shoreline.

Jim Gallagher
Enola, Pennsylvania

73. WIND DIRECTION

Keep your feeder decoys pointed into the wind and your sentinels facing out on the edge of your spread when hunting geese on fields.

Michael Lopreste
Norwich, New York

74. FROZEN UP

Don't fret when your decoys freeze unexpectedly. In the early morning light, waterfowl can see your decoys but often can't tell the water has turned to ice until they are in range.

Glenn Vondra
Johnston, Iowa

75. FAKE SNOW

At times during the season when you've received a light snow, the area around your goose pit will melt from body heat and foot traffic, leaving a bare patch that can spook geese. To solve this problem, I cover the bare patches with Christmas tree snow that is sold in an aerosol can for about a dollar. I also use it to camouflage pit lids. Remember, the little details can have big results.

Jim Thompson, Jr.
Sioux Falls, South Dakota

76. HAY BALE

When hunting Canada geese on snow-covered fields, bring along a bale of hay. Spread the hay thinly on the ground, then put your decoys on top of it. Passing geese think the birds on the ground have scratched through the layer of snow to feed. When it's cold, geese need to save energy. Therefore, they will decoy readily if they think a flock of geese (your decoys) have already done the dirty work of scratching away the snow obscuring waste grain.

Thomas Venezia
Williston, Vermont

77. FIELD DEKES

Late in the duck season in Nebraska, mallards gang up in large feeding concentrations on the grain fields. As a result, I developed a way to use my water keel decoys as field blocks. I fold a 4-foot piece of No. 9 wire into a double-L shape. I drive the open end into the ground, then firmly wedge the keel of a floater decoy between the closed horizontal wire prong. This way, my water keel decoys rest above the stubble, making them just as visible as field decoys.

PUSH INTO GROUND

Bob Lastovica
Omaha, Nebraska

Guns &
Loads

From punt guns once employed by market gunners to the early Browning repeaters, waterfowlers have favored one model of fowling piece or another for generations. The history of waterfowling guns in America is rich with tales of fine craftsmanship and utilitarian modifications, and the advice that follows will serve you well—whether using a classic double or a modern auto-loader.

78. DISTINGUISHING COLORS

Since the printed ink on some shot shells will eventually fade after prolonged rubbing in a shooting vest, it's a good idea to use a fluorescent paint marker to color code your shells. Such a mark won't rub off and will allow you to quickly identify the shot size and whether or not the pellets are steel or lead, thus helping you avoid future problems afield.

Eric Anhalt
Clarksville, Iowa

79. DRY SHELLS

When heading to the marsh for waterfowling, put your shells in a plastic zip-lock bag. It will keep boxes from getting wet and your shells from getting muddy. Soil and debris will foul any gun—especially autoloaders. Keep the shells in their original box, and then put two or three additional boxes in a large zip-lock bag for transportation. Use smaller bags of shells in your coat pocket—the bags will stay open when filled with shells to allow you to quickly reload.

Kevin Morgan
Woodlands, Texas

80. HANDY CHOKE TUBE WRENCH

If you're stuck in a duck blind without a choke tube wrench, a quarter makes an effective emergency 12-gauge wrench and a dime can be used to loosen or tighten a 20-gauge choke tube.

Rob Terrill
Hudson, New Hampshire

81. RELOADING STEEL SHOT

You can reload steel shot both safely and economically—enjoying shot velocities superior to factory loads. Consistency, however, is important when reloading steel shot—especially heavy goose loads of BBBs, Ts, and Fs.

It's a good idea to count the pellets in each shell as reloaders often don't distribute steel shot well. To quickly count the number of steel pellets you need to put in a load, take a spent primer tray and cut it so that there is one hole for every two pellets needed to fill the shot shell. By using a funnel in a shot shell hull, you will be able to quickly fill the hull. Then, you're ready to crimp the shell and repeat the process.

Richard Frye
Clio, Michigan

82. GUN CLEANING

Waterfowlers know well the difficulties of keeping a gun clean. Two helpful items are a 1/2-inch paint brush and a can of compressed air (the canisters are available from photography shops). The paint brush has longer bristles than tooth brushes and, when used in tandem with compressed air, allows you to remove debris from even the most difficult-to-reach areas.

Jeff Poland
Coshocton, Ohio

83. STARTING RIGHT

It is always wise to help beginning duck hunters gain practical experience before their inaugural hunt. Using a portable skeet thrower, try to creatively present them with shots similar to those they will encounter while duck hunting. Also, have them shoot while wearing their hunting coat. Realistic shooting practice will help beginners gain confidence, resulting in better success in the field.

Martin Robillard
Calgary, Alberta

84. SHOOTING STEEL

When shooting steel shot loads, forget about using full chokes and long-barreled shotguns. Steel shot loads form a much tighter shot string, and the muzzle velocities are normally faster. Try a 26-inch barrel and improved cylinder choke—it'll improve your shooting success.

Steve Cherry
Rogers, Arkansas

85. SALT SOLUTION

When hunting waterfowl in salt water, always carry a rust inhibitor and a dry rag with you to the field. Salt water is so corrosive that it will begin damaging the metal parts of your gun almost as soon as it comes in contact with them. Apply the rust inhibitor to your gun immediately after wiping off any water that may have splashed on your gun. If your gun is dunked or heavily doused with salt water, be sure to disassemble it after hunting and run hot water over it to remove all the salt from the metal. A thin coating of gun oil should then be applied to all metal parts of the gun.

Gary Wilson
Poynette, Wisconsin

86. SHELL BOX AND MORE

An old army surplus 50-caliber ammo box is a handy way to store extra shotgun shells for the waterfowling season. You can also keep extra decoy line, decoy anchors, batteries, calls, film, and tools in these waterproof containers.

Stan Chapin II
Celina, Ohio

GARY COX

Retrievers

A morning in the blind just isn't the same without the company of a faithful dog. While well-trained retrievers help us recover more birds, they're more than practical assets. For many hunters, watching a favorite dog negotiate the currents to fetch a downed bird is the highlight of the hunt. No matter how cold it might be, or what time of the morning you might awake, a retriever will always be ready for a day in the blind.

87. FIRST AID KIT

It's a good idea to carry several first aid supplies with you in case you or your dog is injured while afield. I always carry the following items: hydrogen peroxide, Betadine solution swabs, sponge dressings to cover cuts and other wounds, 2-inch-wide gauze bandages to hold dressings in place, first aid tape, a tourniquet, and Neosporin antibiotic ointment. Feel free to add any items to this list that you think might be worthwhile, or check with your veterinarian for other recommendations.

David McEacharn
Delhi, Louisiana

88. FULLY VESTED

When selecting a neoprene vest for your retriever, be sure to order one that fits your dog snugly. Your dog's legs might become entangled in a loose-fitting vest.

Curt Czaplicki
Antioch,Illinois

89. CRANE CAUTION

When hunting sandhill cranes, always make certain a downed bird is indeed dead before attempting to pick it up. A crane's bill is a combination spike and steak knife that can be dangerous. A dog should never be sent to retrieve a crane under any circumstances.

G.K. Chambers
Troup,Texas

90. CHARGED UP

When hunting in a blind with an inexperienced dog, make certain your gun is secured so your dog can't knock it over. It's best to keep your dog under control at all times, but that isn't always possible with young dogs, so secure your shotgun to avoid a shooting accident.

Phil Brodbeck,
Hartland, Wisconsin

91. RETRIEVING GEESE

Training dogs to retrieve and carry a heavy goose can be difficult. To give your dog some practice, try using a

POUR IN SAND
OR LEAD STRAP
SINKERS

CUT SLIT

weighted dummy. To do this, take a plastic dummy, slit the bottom, add sand or lead sinkers, and tape the bottom shut. As your dog becomes more comfortable carrying a heavy load, gradually increase the weight of the dummy until you're confident your dog can handle the heft of a goose. To permanently seal the dummy, use plastic cement that is available at most hardware stores.

William L. Streitz
Roseburg, Oregon

92. DOG SNACKS

By occasionally feeding your retriever small snacks—especially during cold, wet, and heavy work periods—your dog will stay warmer and happier and, consequently, will perform better during the hunt.

Kim Gugisberg, DVM
Glenwood, Minnesota

93. HEAT STRESS

Since most preseason dog training is done in warm weather, make sure you are familiar with early symptoms of heat prostration and hypoglycemia (low blood sugar). Beware of these symptoms: unsteadiness, confusion, weakness, and unusually dark red gums. Early detection and prompt first aid will lessen the likelihood of fatal or long-lasting consequences.

Kim Gugisberg, DVM
Glenwood, Minnesota

94. WHO'S IN CHARGE?

When hunting with a friend and his dog, never give the dog commands unless your friend says it's all right. Dogs may become confused by more than one person giving them commands, so avoid barking commands to another's dog.

Keith Gilbertson
DeForest, Wisconsin

95. DOG REST

If you hunt in shallow water with a retriever, a plastic milk crate makes a great dog stand. Contact your local grocery store or supermarket to see if they have extra milk crates. You can even cover them with camo paint and wire a flat piece of camo-painted wood on top to give your dog a comfortable place to sit next to you.

Kyle Omstead
Tulsa, Oklahoma

Safety

Although waterfowling is safer statistically than playing baseball, the sport isn't without its perils. In addition to the obvious dangers of handling firearms, waterfowlers also must contend with bitter cold temperatures, inclement weather, and boating and wading hazards. Despite these risks, waterfowlers can reduce the element of danger from their hunts by taking a few simple precautions and using common sense.

96. UTILITY HOOK

Having a gun fall over in a blind is not only dangerous, it's hard on the gun's finish. Rather than cutting notches in the side of my blind, I have installed utility hooks next to the bench so I can securely rest my shotgun within easy reach. I buy plastic-coated hooks with screw threads that can be twisted firmly into place by hand without tools. Install other utility hooks in your blind to hang calls, a camera, or anything else you don't want to get wet on the floor of a blind.

Leonard Berkel
St. Charles, Missouri

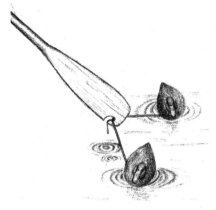

97. SAFE RETRIEVAL

I find that reaching out of a canoe to pick up decoys can be hazardous. Consequently, I cut a notch in one of my paddles to help retrieve my decoys in a safer manner. Simply reach out your paddle and snag your decoy lines with the notch in the paddle. This can be done almost without missing a stroke.

John Oliveira, Jr.
Chicopee, Massachusetts

98. BOATING SAFETY

In my experience, very few waterfowlers consider themselves to be boaters. However, we go out in small boats in every type of weather most others would avoid. Every big water hunter should do the following:
-carry flotation devices
-carry a compass and waterproof matches
-take a boating safety course
-carry day and night emergency flares
-have running lights on your boat
-invest in a handheld, two-way radio
-monitor a marine weather forecast.

Rick Mosback
New Milford, Connecticut

99. REFRESHER COURSE

When it comes time for your Greenwing to take a hunter safety course, retake it along with him or her. It's a great refresher, it shows a desire to be involved with your child, and it proves by example that gun safety and hunting ethics are an integral part of your adventures afield.

Tom Caine
Ridgefield, Washington

100. LIFE LINE

Most states require that all boats carry an approved flotation device for each person on board. In addition to this, I carry a flotation device attached to 50 feet of stout, plastic rope. The cushion can be thrown to someone who has gone overboard, and if the cushion doesn't reach the swimmer on the first throw, the rope  will enable you to retrieve it for another toss. This tip could help save a life, since it isn't wise to try to rescue someone by swimming or wading in frigid water or current.

Steve Rodgers
Paragould, Arkansas

101. BUG OUT

We have several wood duck boxes mounted on steel poles on a pond in northern Minnesota. We used to clean out the houses in late summer after the ducklings had left. We changed our minds after discovering hornet and wasp nests inside some of the boxes. Now we empty and put fresh sawdust in them just before ice-out. We have continued to get excellent wood duck use from our boxes without having any insect problems.

Robert Snyder
Minneapolis, Minnesota

102. HOOK 'EM

Picking up decoys in a boat in deep water can be a
dangerous, trying experience. To prevent my hunting
partners and myself from flipping the boat, I use an 8-
foot closet pole with a screw hook on the end to help
pick up our decoys. After snagging a decoy, I pass it back
to a partner sitting in the middle of the boat. Safety on
windy, wavy days is all-important.

George Pashley
Alpena, Michigan

103. QUICKSAND

When hunting coastal areas, be aware that tidal creeks
and muddy gorges, sometimes called "tidal guts,"
frequently contain quicksand after a receding tide.
While crossing one of these muddy chasms, watch for
level places on the ordinarily steep banks; these are
danger zones, usually characterized by a sheen of
moisture betraying the presence of a quagmire below.

If you find yourself caught in quicksand or sucking
mud, don't panic. If you can't escape by the time you
are up to your crotch, immediately lean forward into
the water and mud and assume a swimming posture.
Your feet and legs will slowly rise as the vacuum suction
is released, allowing you to swim across the surface to
safety. I have freed myself twice on treacherous Alaskan
tidal flats using this method.

Steve Dawson
Dillon, Montana

104. SURVIVAL PAIL

Since I hunt from a canoe, I worry about surviving a
dunking in bitter cold weather. Consequently, I carry a
survival pail in my canoe which also doubles as a seat
in the marsh. It is a 5-gallon discarded plastic paint
pail with a handle and lid. I place a large plastic
garbage bag in the pail for a liner and fill it with the
following: mittens, short boots, sweater, wool shirt,
balaclava, wool socks, thermal underwear, ski warm-up
pants, a space blanket, and whatever else I can cram
inside. It is very important not to snap the cover shut
because you will never be able to get the cover off
when you're soaking wet. Wrap the edge of the lid
with duct tape and make a loop at the end to enable
you to easily remove the lid when you're cold. Always

secure the pail to the canoe so it won't float away if
you capsize.

Peter Cirba
Johnson City, New York

105. CELLULAR PHONE

For solo, old, or out-of-shape
hunters, carrying a cellular phone
along while waterfowling
can be a lifesaver. It can also
bring peace of mind to your
spouse. I used my cellular
phone in the blind on
Horicon Marsh last fall and
had excellent reception.

Henry Felski
Chicago, Illinois

106. WADING STAFF

Always carry a wading staff when setting decoys
or picking up downed birds. A good staff enables you to
check for holes or snags while wading.

Mark Laurent
Taylor Springs, Illinois

Tactics

Waterfowling demands more of hunters than simply being able to call, shoot, and place decoys. Waterfowlers must also know when and where to find ducks and geese under a variety of conditions. Invariably, the most successful waterfowl hunters have developed specialized tactics for hunting the species found in their region.

107. DON'T DOUBLE

Many of us probably have been in a situation where two or more hunters in a blind have shot at the same bird in a flock. It seems to happen most often when individuals are hunting together for the first time. You can lessen your chances of doubling up with a little planning at the beginning of the hunt. My hunting buddies and I divide up each flock of ducks according to our position in the blind and the wind direction. For example, if three of us are hunting, the hunter at the upwind end of the blind shoots at birds in the front of the flock, the hunter in the middle shoots at birds in the middle of the flock, and the hunter at the downwind end of the blind shoots at birds in the back of the flock. If ducks approach the blind head-on, hunters should select birds in relation to their position in the blind: left, right, or center. Dividing up the flock makes it easier to sort out bagged ducks and avoid missed opportunities. However, drawing straws might be necessary for that lone greenhead that shows up first!

Tim Grace
Columbia, Missouri

108. LET 'EM GO

You've come upon your favorite pothole on a blustery late fall day. You peek over the rushes and see 75 mallards and wigeon dabbling. Should you take them as they flush, or just let them go and enjoy the sight? Chances are you will bag more birds if you choose the second option. Obviously, they like the spot, and by not shooting at them, they will return.

Quickly throw out your decoys and take cover. More than likely, they will start coming back in small groups within a few minutes. Granted, it's hard not to shoot

when discovering a large group of birds, but your patience will pay off. It has many times for me.

Don Walsh
La Crosse, Wisconsin

109. STIR IT UP

Ever find yourself sitting over a great decoy spread only to have nothing flying? Well don't just sit there. Stir the pot. Send at least one person out to jump shoot in the surrounding marsh. The jumped ducks will look for a safe haven, and your spread might be the place they choose.

David Chapman
Rock Springs, Wyoming

110. SIMPLE ADVICE

When hunting white-fronted geese in winter ground cover such as rye grass or winter wheat, don't use too many decoys because the geese will probably have become wary of large spreads after several months of hunting pressure. A dozen or less is fine. Many times you can do very well not using any decoys at all, especially if the geese are feeding in the field on a regular basis. Just call a couple of notes till they hear you, then refrain from calling again unless they begin to drift. Often they will glide right to the call's place of origin—you.

Kenny Hebert
Lake Charles, Louisiana

111. MEMORY AID

D abbling ducks typically land short of the decoys.
E arly season—use more hens than drakes.
C alling will add realism to your decoys.
O ffer the birds an inviting opening to land.
Y ou should keep puddler and diver decoys separate.
I nsure that ducks can land into the wind over your
   spread.
N asty, windy weather is a duck hunter's best friend.
G o where the birds are.

Chuck Kartak
Center City, Minnesota

112. SCOUT FIRST

Preparation is the key to successful waterfowling. For every hour spent hunting, an hour should be spent scouting to find where ducks and geese feed, rest, loaf, and seek refuge and what their flight patterns are between these areas.

Chuck Kartak
Center City, Minnesota

113. ON THE SIDE

Don't place your decoys immediately upwind of your blind. Instead, place them slightly off to one side so the movements of dogs and hunters won't be as noticeable when ducks are circling the decoys.

Chuck Kartak
Center City, Minnesota

114. HONEY HOLES

Late in the season when ducks get gun- and blind-shy, don't overlook scouting small, isolated bodies of water such as farm ponds and irrigation ditches. Ducks will often spend the day on these honey holes and return to a marsh to roost after sunset.

Kenny Hebert
Lake Charles, Louisiana

115. DIVER DOWN

While pursuing crippled diving ducks, row upwind of the spot where the duck dove last. This will give you the advantage of having the wind at your back when the duck surfaces. Also, try to keep the boat in a position so the duck will surface to the left if the shooter is right-handed or to the right if the shooter is left-handed.

Patrick Horvath
Greenfield, Wisconsin

116. RANGE FINDER

To determine the correct distance to shoot ducks over decoys, try this method. Before the season opens, I place an old piece of cane pole 30 yards in front of my blind. I measure the distance using a length of string, 32 yards long. Once the season opens, the first thing I do in the morning is find my marker and place my favorite over-sized bluebill decoy beside it. Then, I place my spread around it. This is a simple way to ensure that any decoying ducks will be within proper killing range. This has helped us keep crippling losses near zero for a number of seasons.

Patrick Horvath
Greenfield, Wisconsin

117. TILL DARK

When hunting snow geese, scouting is the most important factor determining success or failure. Many hunters go out in midafternoon, find a field full of geese, and decide to set up there the next morning. However, the geese may clean out the grain on the field before sunset and move on. Consequently, watch geese until they leave the field to roost at dark. In the morning, they will always return to the place where they fed last.

Pete Ressler
Bismarck, North Dakota

118. ASTUTE OBSERVATION

When doing your preliminary scouting the night before a hunt, take notice of what direction ducks are flying into the pond to roost. Ducks will usually fly out of a marsh in the same direction from which they arrived. This will help you determine where to place your decoys and blind, especially on small bodies of water. Be careful not to spook ducks while entering the marsh and setting up in the early morning darkness.

Terry Price
Monroe, North Carolina

119. MUD HEN

Slow day in the blind? Don't overlook the inglorious coot to fill slow times in the blind and grace the dinner table. After bagging a few, breast the birds, soak the breasts for a few hours in your favorite game marinade, and prepare them on the grill. Although they don't taste like chicken, they can be quite palatable after a cold day of hunting.

Jeff Lawrence
Oxford, Mississippi

120. COUP DE GRACE

If you don't have a retriever, never hesitate to shoot a
crippled bird on the water once more, even if it appears
to be mortally wounded. Too many "dead" birds have
swum away.

Jeff Lawrence
Oxford, Mississippi

121. OPEN HOLE

When you find your favorite shallow water hole has
frozen, don't despair. If the ice is less than 2 inches thick,
break it into large sheets with a paddle. Then push the
broken sheets under the ice on the edges of the opening.
In short order, you can clear a large hole that will attract
ducks like a magnet.

Wilson Burton, Jr.
Brentwood, Tennessee

122. OTHER SIDE

When hunting a narrow body of water 50 or 60 yards
wide, put your decoys on the far side of the slough.
Ducks will naturally land on the outside edge of the
decoys, closer to your blind.

Wilson Burton, Jr.
Brentwood, Tennessee

123. OLD ADVICE

When hunting ducks in an area that has both flooded
timber and fields, follow the old-timers' advice and hunt
the timber when it's sunny and fields when it's cloudy.

Larry Reid
Alton, Illinois

124. FICKLE WIND

If you expect the wind to change while you are hunting,
try putting out three or four groups of decoys to cover
any possible wind change and keep yourself from having
to move decoys while the birds are flying.

Scott Sommerlatte
Lake Jackson, Texas

Waders

Modern waders have forever altered the definition of comfort in a duck marsh. While many waterfowlers still favor the venerable loose-fitting rubber models of yesteryear, others have embraced the invention of form-fitting neoprenes. No matter your fancy, however, the following tips will help you repair, store, and better use your waders.

125. FINDING LEAKS

Instead of filling your hip boots or chest waders with water to detect leaks, take them into a dark room, insert a flashlight in the waders, and look for tiny rays of light shining through the holes. Once you've found a hole, mark the spot and repair it with a standard repair kit.

Troy Herrin and Dave Spellman III
Houston, Texas

126. WADER REPAIR

For an efficient way to repair your leaky waders, try taking them to a reliable tire repair shop. Such a place will typically have the proper tools and equipment to fix the leak both effectively and cheaply.

Matthew L. Johnson
Lawrence, Kansas

127. WARM FEET

The best way to keep your feet warm in waders is to spray them with antiperspirant powder spray, wear a wick sock (silk or polypropyene) as a liner, followed by a heavy, wool sock. To keep your pant legs from sliding up as you place your feet in your waders, cut 3 or 4 inches off the top of an old pair of socks. Place these "ankle bands" on the outside of your pant legs before you get into your waders.

Michael J. Peal
East Moline, Illinois

128. BAG IT

It's a good idea to keep your hunting license, wallet, and small camera in a sealable plastic bag inside your waders. Should you swamp your waders, at least these items won't get wet or lost.

Blake E. Matray
Skandia, Michigan

129. WADER STORAGE

When the hunting season is finished and you're through
using your waders for the season, clean them
thoroughly, removing all dirt and debris. Next, hang
them upside down for storage in a cool, dry place.
Finally, spray them with a light coating of Armor All
Protectant®. This will keep your rubber waders from
drying out and cracking, thus ensuring that they'll keep
you dry next season.

Michael J. Pentland
Waterford, Pennsylvania

130. OVER YOUR HEAD

When wearing standard, old-fashioned rubber waders, it
is a good idea to wear a wading belt like those sold in
outdoor catalogs. Should you take a spill, the belt will
keep most of the water above your waist, which will
keep your lower body dry. However, be sure your belt has
a quick-release buckle and to wear your suspenders
outside your clothing so you can shed your waders if
necessary.

Allen Kent
Clarksdale, Mississippi

131. ONE SIZE FITS ALL

If you want to keep an extra pair of waders around for a
friend or family member to use while hunting, but want
a pair that will fit almost anyone, buy a pair of extra-
large stocking-foot neoprene waders. The neoprenes are
very elastic in nature and will fit snugly from the very
slim to the heavy person. Virtually anyone you take
hunting will be able to fit their feet inside size 12 boots.
Don't worry even if they have very small feet, because
the suction created when the rubber boots fill with water
will form-fit the waders to their feet and allow them to
have traction, even on slick mud bottoms.

Cameron Jones
Fort Worth, Texas

132. BOOT DRYER

For an inexpensive way to dry out the inside of your waders, simply use one of the old-style hair dryers with the long, flexible hose and bag attachment. Just remove the bag and run the hose down to the foot of the wader, and you'll have dry boots in no time. You can find these dryers occasionally at garage sales and secondhand shops for less than five dollars.

Bradley V. Schultz
Lindstom, Minnesota

133. NEOPRENE FOR WARMTH

When hunting in cold weather, don't forget to wear your neoprene waders—even if you're not going to be standing in water. Neoprenes of 4 or 5 millimeters will keep you toasty during even the nastiest conditions.

Don Janoff
Northampton, Massachusetts

134. FAST REPAIR

If you tear a hole in your waders when you don't have access to a repair kit, simply patch it with strips of duct tape. Tape two or three strips over the tear on both the inside and outside of the waders. This will keep your waders from leaking until you have time to get them properly patched.

Scott Jackson
Jefferson, Georgia

135. BONE DRY

To dry out the inside of your waders or hip boots, use 3- or 4-inch PVC pipe. Place the PVC pipe inside the boots and turn them upside down. The pipe will allow air to circulate, and your boots will dry overnight.

Jack McNeely
Lake Charles, Louisiana

136. FOOT LOOSE

If you have trouble with your feet pulling out of your waders when walking in mud, cut 1 1/2-inch sections of old inner tube and slip them over your boots, around your ankles. Then, pull the tube strips away from your ankle and give them a half twist, tucking the opening over your toes and back underneath the heel. This will hold your feet in the boots in the deepest sludge.

Robert Bayless III
Phoenix, Arizona

Miscellaneous Tips

You won't want to miss this treasure trove of information that's sure to make you a better waterfowler. While we didn't have separate categories for these tips, the following advice was too good to pass up.

137. SOLID FOOTING

If you're uncomfortable shooting from a canoe and prefer to stash the craft and hunt in the cattails or rushes, a good way to provide yourself with a flat place from which to shoot is to use a flat board or stackable bread rack. Since it can be tricky to shoot with your feet stuck in the mud, such a platform will give you more mobility when shooting.

Jim Williams
Penn Run, Pennsylvania

138. PERSONAL HEATER

For the long, cold days in the blind, you can use a large coffee can filled with charcoal as an effective heater. Fill the can half full with charcoal and saturate the briquets with lighter fluid—or use a brand of charcoal that doesn't require it. When lit, the coals should provide enough heat to get you through the midday lull. This heater can also double as a stove. Make six 1/2-inch holes near the top of the can and set your frying pan right on top. Remember to save the lid so you can transport the ashes after the can cools.

Paul Schoenberger
St. Louis, Missouri

139. RECOVERING BIRDS

When hunting waterfowl in a marsh with or without a dog, it's a good idea to carry a compass to mark fallen birds. By taking a compass reading on a downed duck, you'll greatly increase your chances of finding it.

Carl D. Gutierrez
Aurora, Illinois

140. DUCK STRINGER

Here's an easy and inexpensive way to make a serviceable stringer for carrying waterfowl. You'll need a strip of leather 2 inches wide and 6 inches long and six stout bootlaces. Buy the leather at a craft store, or use an old belt. Be sure to use enough leather to allow for any adjustments you wish to make. Then, punch (or cut) three holes in each end of the leather—making certain they are large enough to thread both ends of the bootlace through. Next, thread the laces through the holes from the rough side of the leather out. Adjust the lengths, knot, and trim. Melt trimmed ends with a match to prevent fraying. The six loops can then be used to "string" your birds by placing their necks or feet through the loops. The rough side of the leather provides a slip-resistant surface for over-the-shoulder transporting from the blind to your vehicle. The stringer is strong enough to transport six geese, leaving your hands free to carry a gun, pack, or flashlight.

Will Martin
Austin, Texas

141. CLEANING TOOL

For hunters like me who hunt geese where there is lots of mud, a bathroom variety toilet scrubber is a must. Use the scrubber to clean the mud off goose shells and stakes at the end of each hunt. This will ensure that your decoys will be clean and ready to go the next time you go. The brush can also be used to clean the mud off your boots, the floor of your blind, and the floor mats of your hunting vehicle.

Lance R. Crawford
Delano,Tennessee

142. DRY GLOVES

If you're tired of getting your gloves and hands all wet while waterfowling, try using a pair of surgical gloves. While working with decoys in the water, place these plastic coverings over your regular gloves, and your hands will remain both warm and dry.

Jesse Mason
Chalmette, Louisiana

143. TROPHY TIPS

A great way to blow the dust off your game and bird mounts is to switch the hose of your vacuum cleaner to the return hole and blow the dust right off the fur and feathers. This is a great time-saver that will keep your mounts looking lifelike.

Susan Swetnam
Bowie, Maryland

144. STAMP DILEMMA

If you commonly hunt waterfowl in more than one state, consider signing your Federal Migratory Bird Stamp—the stamp you'll need to hunt in every state— and having it laminated. Once it's laminated, punch a hole in one end of the plastic and attach the stamp to your waterfowling jacket using a metal ring. Whenever you go waterfowling, you'll have your federal stamp with you.

Richard F. Kress
Rahway, New Jersey

145. HEADS UP

Any hunter who has spent time lying on stubble fields while waterfowl hunting knows how important it is to be comfortable, since you can't hunt long if your head and neck are sore. A way to be more comfortable while lying down is to use a dock bumper as a headrest. Not only will it allow you to remain more comfortable for longer periods of time, it will also help you see incoming birds better. The bumpers are light, waterproof, inexpensive, and readily available.

Mark W. Zagger
Syracuse, New York

146. BACK SUPPORT

If you've ever hunted where you must stand in the water for several hours, you know how tired your back can become—especially if you're wearing waders with suspenders. A way to avoid back strain is to wear a back support belt—the kind often worn by construction and warehouse workers. Without the back strain, you can remain afield far longer and extend your enjoyment while hunting.

Ken Hamil
Atlanta, Georgia

147. A LEG UP

When hunting in flooded timber for long periods of time, your legs will often become tired. To avoid this, attach a tree stand—the kind often used by deer hunters—to a tree and have a seat. Then, you'll have a comfortable and secure place to sit. You can find tree stands in most sporting goods stores.

Hamilton Kemp
Little Rock, Arkansas

148. THE REAL SECRET

It's good to know how to call, decoy, and shoot ducks, but the best way to get birds is to go often and stay late!

Richard B. Feucht II
Ville Platte, Louisiana

149. CAN YOU SPARE A GUN?

If you're planning an extended waterfowling foray, be sure to take an extra gun along. You may need it!

Gary A. Green
Lynchburg, Virginia

150. WALKING STICK

When hiking through a marsh, try using a ski pole or other stick to help you maintain your balance—it just may keep you from getting wet.

Jackie Frisque
Larsen, Wisconcin

151. FEATHERS AND FLIES

Fully utilize the resource by saving your duck and goose skins. You may be able to give your waterfowl skins to a flyfishing friend or to your local tackle shop. (Selling or bartering feathers, however, is illegal.) Some skins are more valuable than others to flytiers, so check to see which they prefer.

J.L. Abbott
Norcross, Georgia

152. TAXIDERMY TIP

When placing a bird in the freezer before taking it to a taxidermist, do not wrap it in newspaper. Newspaper will draw the moisture from the skin and increase the chances of freezer burn. Instead, apply a damp cloth to the feet and place the carcass in a double plastic bag before putting it in the freezer. Don't forget to tag your waterfowl—it's the law!

John Scagline
Monongahela, Pennsylvania

153. TRAVELING MAGAZINES

We've all waited for long periods in doctors' or dentists' offices and have often found the magazines there to be of little interest. A great way to promote waterfowl conservation and hunting is to take a copy of *Ducks Unlimited* magazine to the office with you and share some valuable information.

Loren Fellows
Lincoln, Nebraska

154. PICKED CLEAN

Many waterfowlers like to pick their ducks in the blind while they wait for more birds to pass by. It's a good way to avoid making a mess back home. However, be sure to heed federal regulations and leave a head and/or a wing attached to the carcass until you get home.

John Drees
Carroll, Iowa

155. LOOK, MOM, WARM HANDS

By placing a hand warmer in the pockets of your shooting jacket, you can keep from having to wear gloves while hunting on cold days. This will allow you to handle your gun better, increasing the odds of taking birds.

Phil Dunne
Geneva, Illinois

156. DRY HANDS

When hunting in frigid temperatures, try wearing a pair of neoprene waterproof gloves when handling the decoys. When you're finished, replace the neoprene gloves with your warmer gloves which will still be dry.

Terry Gilbertson
Phillips, Wisconsin

157. REFLECTIONS ON GLASSES

Wearing eyeglasses while hunting can be a real disadvantage as light reflection from your glasses may alert waterfowl. To avoid this, try wearing glasses with flat-black frames and nonreflective lenses. The nonreflective lenses are made by treating them with a series of special coatings. Check with your optician for these services.

Douglas Domedian
Medina, New York

158. FREE ADVICE

Never criticize a friend's dog—even if he asks for it!

Stan Chapin II
Celina, Ohio

159. HOW OLD IS THAT GOOSE?

Geese are easy to age. Simply look at their tail feathers. Juvenile geese have a "V" notch at the tip of their tail feathers. Adult geese, however, have a rounded or pointed tip on their tail feathers.

Fran Gough
Macungie, Pennsylvania

160. FOR THE MEMORIES

Along with your gun, shells, and other essential waterfowling gear, consider taking along a camera and tape recorder on your next waterfowling junket. As you get older, you might find that you enjoy your photos and tapes of past hunts very much.

Ramsey Falconer
Houston, Texas

161. SUPPORT DU

One of the best tips to improve your waterfowling is to support Ducks Unlimited and to convince others to do the same. No other organization in America has done more to preserve waterfowl habitat and our waterfowling legacy. Through your attendance at local DU fund-raising events and volunteer work, you can make a significant contribution to the future of waterfowling.

DU Magazine Staff
Memphis, Tennessee

HELP SPREAD THE WORD ABOUT DUCKS UNLIMITED. BECAUSE MORE MEMBERS TODAY MEANS MORE WATERFOWL TOMORROW.

PAYMENT METHOD

☐ Check or money order

☐ Visa ☐ MasterCard

☐ American Express ☐ Discover

SEND TO:
Ducks Unlimited, Inc.,
One Waterfowl Way, Memphis, TN 38120

☐ **$20 Regular Member** ☐ **$10 Greenwing (0-18 yrs.)** ☐ **$200 Sponsor**

Credit Card # _____ Exp. Date _____

Signature _____

Name _____

Address _____

City_____ State _____ Zip Code _____

For Greenwing Memberships: Birth date _____

For office use only ▶ TIPS94	*MEMBER NO.*	*AMOUNT*	*TYPE*

©Copyright Ducks Unlimited, Inc., 1994
NOTE: Your membership contribution is tax-deductible except for the $3 value of DUCKS UNLIMITED magazine and $3 value of other membership fulfillment items to the amount allowed by law.

HELP SPREAD THE WORD ABOUT DUCKS UNLIMITED. BECAUSE MORE MEMBERS TODAY MEANS MORE WATERFOWL TOMORROW.

PAYMENT METHOD

☐ Check or money order

☐ Visa ☐ MasterCard

☐ American Express ☐ Discover

SEND TO:
Ducks Unlimited, Inc.,
One Waterfowl Way, Memphis, TN 38120

☐ **$20 Regular Member** ☐ **$10 Greenwing (0-18 yrs.)** ☐ **$200 Sponsor**

Credit Card # _____ Exp. Date _____

Signature _____

Name _____

Address _____

City_____ State _____ Zip Code _____

For Greenwing Memberships: Birth date _____

For office use only ▶ TIPS94	*MEMBER NO.*	*AMOUNT*	*TYPE*

©Copyright Ducks Unlimited, Inc., 1994
NOTE: Your membership contribution is tax-deductible except for the $3 value of DUCKS UNLIMITED magazine and $3 value of other membership fulfillment items to the amount allowed by law.